The Beautiful Old Houses of Quebec

P. ROY WILSON   with a foreword by JEAN PALARDY

The Beautiful Old Houses of Quebec

UNIVERSITY OF TORONTO PRESS   TORONTO AND BUFFALO

© University of Toronto Press 1975
Toronto and Buffalo
Printed in Canada

Library of Congress Cataloging in Publication Data

Wilson, P. Roy, 1900-
    The beautiful old houses of Quebec.

    Includes index.
    1. Architecture, Domestic - Quebec (Province)
    I. Title.
    NA7242.Q3W54   971.4   75-8501
    ISBN 0-8020-2146-8

The publication of this book has been assisted by the Canada Council.

Contents

Foreword

I am very happy to have the opportunity to write this foreword to Roy Wilson's book, not only because I consider him a friend, but also, and especially, because of the respect and admiration I feel for the research and studies he has carried out, and continues to carry out, in a field about which I feel so deeply. The title he has chosen identifies beauty with the old houses of Quebec, and the preservation of that beauty is one of my constant concerns. Indeed it is essential, I am certain, that our country should come to recognize the need to save these witnesses of our past and of our civilization. But even beyond this, who can help but respond to the grace of a lovely old house of harmonious proportions?

For several years now I have been in a position to appreciate the sketches, watercolours, plans, and elevations of the old houses of Quebec which Roy Wilson has created tirelessly and patiently; he has built a fine work, inspired by the past architecture of our land. As an architect himself he has been captivated by the innate sense of proportion which our builders, carpenters, and masons of yesteryear possessed. One need only tour the Île d'Orléans and examine the lovely façades of its old homes to understand his enthusiasm. In spite of a certain assymetry – doors uncentred, for example, and windows spaced unequally apart – the overall effect is delightful, and the very assymetry, instead of spoiling the façades, on the contrary enhances their originality and charm. Rare are the architects today who would dare to gamble on the design of a façade with as much inventiveness and freedom. Our forebears were sufficiently in command of their craft to have no need for submission to a strict set of precepts, especially in the planning of a simple dwelling. For them, in building a rural home, the golden section could be a guide, but never an inflexible master. The results prove how right they were.

Roy Wilson began to assemble an important record of our rural houses when he became a student of architecture. For many years he has spent the summers travelling across the Province with the intention of measuring the old homes, of sketching them, and of noting the characteristic details of their construction. A large number of his measured drawings have been deposited in the Public Archives of Canada, where they may be consulted by researchers and interested laymen.

From 1930 to 1943, he was responsible for a course at the School of Architecture at McGill University, when Professor Ramsay Traquair was its head. During that period he frequently accompanied his students on summer trips in the neighbourhood of Montreal and of Quebec, and along the two shores of the lower St. Lawrence. He helped and advised them in the practical work which was part of their studies – making plans and elevations of churches, houses, and other venerable buildings.

Between 1938 and 1940, in collaboration with Clarence Gagnon, the famous Canadian artist, he built a model of a Quebec village which can still be seen today, although damaged, in the Musée de Vaudreuil. The model depicted a village of the past which, it was hoped, would be built on Mount Royal; but, alas, the plan was never implemented. I retain the hope that someday the project will become a reality, for it would be well worth while.

The illustrations contained in this volume represent only a tiny part of the record that has been accumulated by its author over the course of years. They give, however, an overall view of the old architecture of our Province.

I wish for this book all the success it deserves. It will give all who love old houses an opportunity to deepen their understanding of them. And if, thanks to this work, some ancient dwellings escape destruction or mutilation, its aim will have been largely achieved.

Jean Palardy, OC

Introduction

The second word of the title of this book is the important one – Beautiful. For centuries the designers of buildings have thought of Beauty as being of equal importance with Function; but in our machine age, when huge buildings are put together in huge precast pieces, with no accent whatever at the corners, till the façade looks like a piece of yard-goods terminated with scissors, Beauty is almost forgotten – Efficiency and Economy are our masters.

Now do not suppose that the designers of the old houses of French-Canada were unconcerned with efficiency and economy. Both these qualities were vital to them. The people were poor, by our standards, and life on a pioneer farm left nothing 'in the kitty' for luxuries. Everything but window-glass was made on the premises. Heavy timbers were axed and boards were sawn out by hand. Roof-trusses were mortised, tenoned, and secured with large oak pegs. Nails were scarce, for they were hand-forged, as were hinges, latches, and shutter hold-backs. Shingles were hand-split cedar and walls were usually built of local stone.

Something more should be said about the walls. The

popular belief is that the first houses in Canada were built of round logs, with notched corners. This is not true. The Norman settlers knew nothing of log cabins. It was the Scandinavians, who came later, who taught this technique. The first settlers from Normandy were used to building *colombage pierotté,* wooden frame with stone in-filling, akin to half-timber, or with solid stone of which there was plenty, especially where stones had to be removed from the land to make it tillable. They had no cement so they used lime-mortar, which had little strength. Such walls had to be of great thickness to furnish the necessary stability by sheer weight. There are records of *colombage* buildings in New France dating from 1644, but they could not withstand the severe Canadian climate, and no important examples remain.

A number of the stone houses appear – on first sight – to be wholly, or partly, of wood. This illusion is an indirect result of the lack of cement-mortar. If left unprotected with exterior wood, the stone walls of houses in exposed positions would soak up driving rain, freeze, and break up. Even chimneys, because of their exceptionally vulnerable position, were thus sheathed in wood, apparently the most illogical material to use where fire is concerned. This no doubt accounted for the usual ladder attached to the roof – ready for immediate use in case of fire. Of course the covering of a colourful stone wall with grey boards detracts somewhat from its monumental quality.

As mentioned before, stone walls needed thickness to assure long life, but weight at the top was undesirable. Consequently walls and chimneys were battered – sloped inwards as they were built, usually about 1½ degrees to the vertical.

In shape, the earliest roofs usually followed their Norman ancestors. The style, known as 'pavilion,' very French in origin, was steep at front and back and steeper still at the ends, with a slight 'bell-cast' at the eaves, and plain wooden finials at the ends of the ridge. The early eaves were of small projection, only nine inches to a foot. The pavilion shape subsequently continued in popularity, probably because of its graceful, pyramidal character. Its ends became so steep that in some instances, such as the Alexandre Gendreau house at St Laurent on Île d'Orléans (page 68), they became almost vertical – in

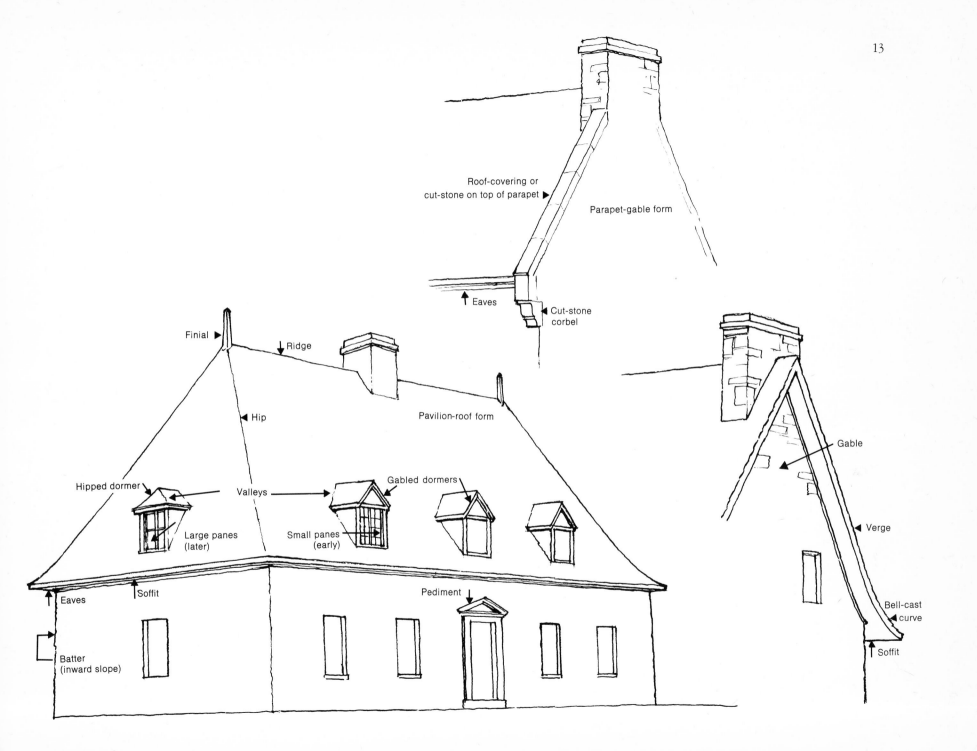

Roof-covering or cut-stone on top of parapet ▶

Parapet-gable form

↑ Eaves

◀ Cut-stone corbel

Finial ▶

↓ Ridge

◀ Hip

Pavilion-roof form

Hipped dormer

Valleys

Gabled dormers

Gable

Large panes (later)

Small panes (early)

Verge

Soffit

Eaves

Pediment

Bell-cast curve

Batter (inward slope)

↑ Soffit

14

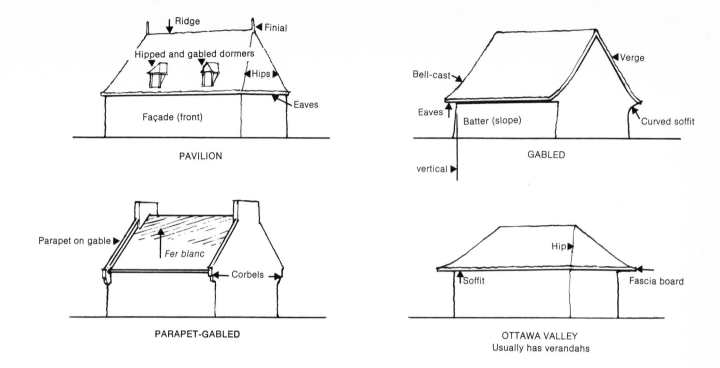

PAVILION

Ridge
Finial
Hipped and gabled dormers
Hips
Eaves
Façade (front)

GABLED

Verge
Bell-cast
Eaves
Batter (slope)
Curved soffit
vertical

PARAPET-GABLED

Parapet on gable
Fer blanc
Corbels

OTTAWA VALLEY
Usually has verandahs

Hip
Soffit
Fascia board

4 BASIC TYPES OF ROOFS

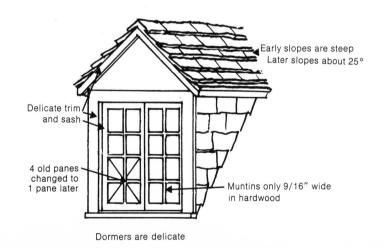

Early slopes are steep
Later slopes about 25°

Delicate trim
and sash

4 old panes
changed to
1 pane later

Muntins only 9/16" wide
in hardwood

Dormers are delicate

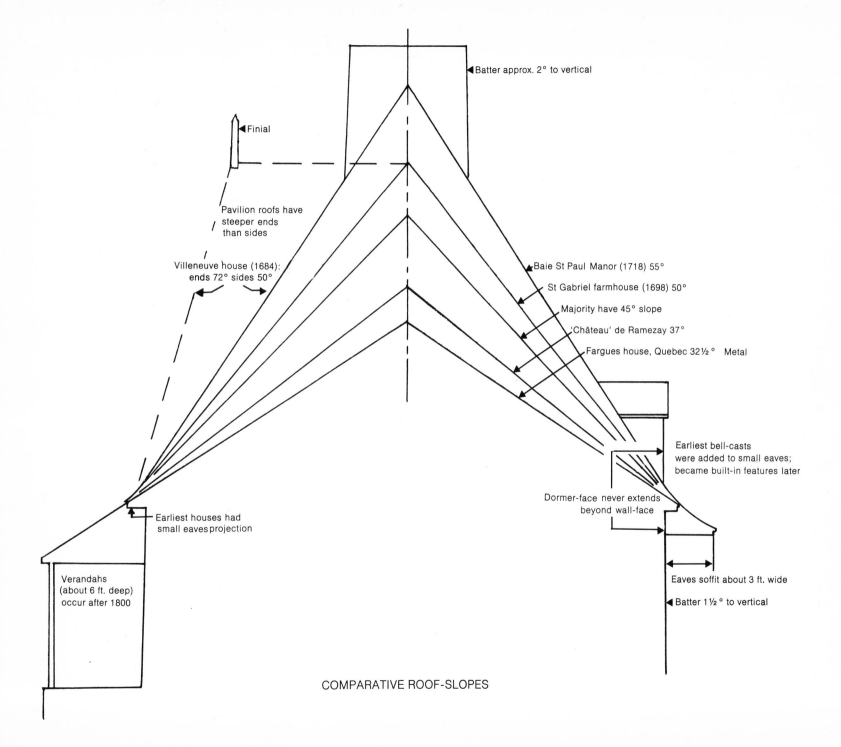

Batter approx. 2° to vertical

Finial

Pavilion roofs have
steeper ends
than sides

Villeneuve house (1684):
ends 72° sides 50°

Baie St Paul Manor (1718) 55°

St Gabriel farmhouse (1698) 50°

Majority have 45° slope

'Château' de Ramezay 37°

Fargues house, Quebec 32½ °   Metal

Earliest bell-casts
were added to small eaves;
became built-in features later

Dormer-face never extends
beyond wall-face

Earliest houses had
small eaves projection

Eaves soffit about 3 ft. wide

Batter 1½ ° to vertical

Verandahs
(about 6 ft. deep)
occur after 1800

COMPARATIVE ROOF-SLOPES

fact battered gables – in which the three dormer windows are in 'bas relief' (and probably were added later, since the earliest houses had no dormers).

Contemporary with pavilion roofs, and more suitable in towns of adjoining houses, was the gabled style. This form allowed two other features, end-chimneys and deep eaves. In a pavilion roof the chimneys look best in the ridge. In the stone-gabled house they are more logical in the end-walls. Here they flourished, until in the 'Château' de Ramezay, a double-depth house with rooms each side of a longitudinal centre-wall, the chimney becomes about two thirds as wide as the house itself. Large chimneys lend a house an air of stability and hospitality, and the end-chimneys of the town houses were much admired. The French habit of placing finials at the ends of the ridge of a pavilion roof – for aesthetic reasons only – was sometimes followed in a gabled house also, as in the small house at St François (page 46). Sometimes the finials became false chimneys – in fact wooden boxes – and in this form are found on many houses on the Île d'Orléans.

The projection of the eaves became bigger and bigger. The habitant began to realize that by increasing the overhang, not only could he better protect the wall below from the elements, but the rooms as well from the scorching summer sun, yet still allow the lower rays of winter to penetrate the house with cheering results. From the aesthetic point of view, the deep shadow cast by big eaves was attractive, especially on a whitewashed wall in sunny weather, and the 'bell-cast' curve at the base of the rafters – though a snow catcher – was a thing of beauty, if part of a parabolic curve. Some painstaking builders even went so far as to install rafters curved from top to bottom, as in the Ulric Drouin house (page 72). Such an effort entailed infinitely more work than merely adding curved out-lookers to the ends of straight rafters, and shows the devotion that even a poor farmer then had to the cause of Beauty.

The next architectural feature to be adopted was the parapet-gable of the mother country. In 1721 half the town of Montreal was destroyed by fire, and in 1734 another fire demolished one third of the town. It was then deemed necessary to pass a law, similar to that of 1673 in Quebec, which required the gable (or end) walls of any house which adjoined another to be carried up about eighteen inches above the roof-surface – and so prevent a fire spreading from roof to roof. This practice was common in both France and England, and now became common even in the rural communities of the new land. The farmers, having seen that the fine, new town houses had parapets, decided to copy them, although they actually served no desirable purpose in an isolated house – and indeed the roof was more liable to leak when it abutted the stone wall of the gable instead of covering it, as in the previous fashion. There were other disadvantages. The eaves-projection could only be about a foot, as in the pavilion version, because it had to butt against the lower end of the parapet. Moreover, the parapet had to be supported on an expensive, moulded, cut-stone corbel or two, as in the Lebeuf or Charest house (page 96), in which the verandah was added later.

The verandah was the next thing to interest the country house builder. We have seen that deep eaves became popular for a number of reasons, and they grew and grew until they had to be supported on a row of posts. The result was a verandah, about six feet wide, with a wooden floor for chair-rocking and other means of neighbourly relaxation. First of all the verandah grew on the front or back of the house, but later it was extended to the sides. This suggested a return to the hipped roof, one with eaves on all four sides. Its pitch was not as steep as that of the pavilion, because it looked more graceful with a flatter slope, like that over the verandahs. The outcome was a long, graceful curve – and the 'Ottawa valley' type was born.

The success of this type is questionable. The rooms become dark, when roofs project seven feet out from every window. Furthermore snow melts on the warm, upper parts of the roof and freezes as it runs out onto the exposed verandah roofs. Subsequent melting snow or rain is stopped on meeting this ice, and backs up under the shingles, causing damage. The flatter the roof-pitch, the more likelihood of such damage.

So much for the four main divisions in the form of French-Canadian houses. Let us now look at the details of their construction, the largest and most important of which is the roof-truss. The early settler was exceptionally careful about the strength of his roof. The farmer-builder of today omits even the ridge-piece, but in the old times the ridge was supported on a five-foot-deep, well-braced truss of hewn timbers, mortised, tenoned, and pegged together, running from gable to gable. Vertical posts incorporated in this truss sometimes extended downwards to form the king-posts of lateral trusses, which rested on and were knee-braced to the wall-plates, front and rear. Rafters, about five feet at most on centres, hewn to about 5″ x 5″ in section, ran from wall-plate to the top of the main truss. The timbers were all axe-hewn to large, well-engineered dimensions, and the resulting framework is so strong that even when four of the six knee-braces of the lateral trusses have been removed – as in the case of the 1688 Hurtubise house (page 32), which was acquired and restored by the Canadian Heritage of Quebec after 270 years – the roof still stands almost intact. Some pavilion roofs were built with a longitudinal truss, and some much larger houses, such as the Trestler house in Dorion (page 62), were built without it.

Fenestration plays an important part in the design of all these houses. Symmetry on the front, with the door in the middle and equally spaced windows each side, was the ideal, but in many cases, particularly in the farmhouses of the Île d'Orléans, where vehicle sheds were often incorporated in the dwelling, this ideal was seldom obtainable. The window-spacing elsewhere in the main storey was generally haphazard, but there was a desire for equality in size, both in window sash and in window panes. Equal-sized panes give a uniformity of scale to a building, even when the frames are of different sizes. Small panes, usually twelve in each casement sash, later gave way to larger ones as they became available – three panes taking the place of twelve. Dormer windows were not common in the early days, since the top storey was not inhabited but was often used as a granary – hence the French word, 'grenier.' But expanding families needed more bedrooms, and dormer windows were added to the roof to light them. Their numbers were altered over the years. Two, as in the Villeneuve house at Charlesbourg (page 30), became three in time, and three, as in the Simon Fraser house at Ste Anne de

Bellevue (page 120), became four. Occasionally there were two storeys in the roof, and therefore two rows of dormers, in which the lower were considerably larger than the upper, indicating greater importance. Dormers were usually equal in spacing, not only because of even spacing of the rafters on which they rested, but because even spacing lends an architectural dignity. Successful house design does not require the dormers to be centred over the lower storey windows. As long as they are tastefully placed and the eaves have a strong projection, the lower windows can be haphazard. Perhaps the projecting mass of a dormer outweighs aesthetically the need for symmetry in the other windows. Old-time dormers were delicate in detail, the eaves and jambs were narrow, and the sash was light. Many a present-day version of a French-Canadian house has been spoiled by heavy, clumsy dormers.

Where there were two or more storeys in the house-wall, a definite attempt was made to place the windows in line, vertically, as in the architect-designed châteaux of old France. In the gable walls there was a considerable tendency to place them symmetrically, or leave them out altogether. Shutters on the lower-storey windows were common. They not only provided protection against thieves, Indian attacks, and the heat of noon-day, but later afforded a chance to use a cheery colour, of which the average French-Canadian had always been fond. Moreover, the double-spiralled wrought-iron shutter-holdbacks were beautiful, as well as functional.

Roof-covering consisted of split shingles at first, but later, in an attempt to prevent the spread of fire from sparks alighting on the roof, flat metal sheets were used. Known as *fer blanc*, these were about 10″ x 12″, laid at about 30 degrees to the horizontal, so that the rain dripped off the point of one on to the upper face of the next. Legend has it that the sheets were originally made by flattening the tins in which tea, bully-beef, and other foodstuffs were imported. As they were inadequately tinned, they became slightly rusty at first, and from a distance looked like gold. Excessive rust later destroyed not only their beauty but their weatherproof quality, so that they had to be painted.

As time went on, houses became more sophisticated. An evenly coursed façade in cut-stone became common, even in the country, and some of those builders who could not afford cut-stone covered the exterior of their houses with planks, with chamfered 'quoins' at the corners to imitate stone. Some dwellings were almost ostentatious, such as the Sabrevois de Bleury manor (page 100), a truly delightful little building which, however, bore no resemblance to the current style of Quebec house. It was destroyed, only about fifteen years ago, by a too-apprehensive government bureau, under the pretext that it might shelter escapees from the nearby St Vincent de Paul penitentiary. The loss is irreparable.

Many other houses, of greater size and dignity, were built by the people of New France. I have only touched on the most common types, on which the larger houses and manors were based. I suggest that the reader study Professor Ramsay Traquair's excellent book, *The Old Architecture of Quebec,* for a more detailed description of the churches and town buildings, remembering the opinion that I heard him express so often, that the most beautiful old buildings of this province are to be found, not in the towns, but in the country. Long may they survive!

This book is an attempt to foster public interest in these lovely houses, an interest which has been sadly lacking, so that hundreds of them have been mutilated beyond hope of redemption, or razed altogether. Unfortunately the lack of cement in the mortar makes destruction – even in the heavy stone walls – comparatively easy, and the temptation to add another storey – instead of another wing – too often irresistible. For some tragic reason, the craftiness of the inventors of artificial stone and imitation brick seems to be so much admired that these false materials have been used by modern builders in preference to honest ones.

If you go in search of these houses, do not expect to recognize them from the illustrations in this book. More frequently than not, they have been changed beyond recognition – roofs have been raised to a flatter slope, windows have been replaced by a sheet of plate-glass, stone walls have been covered with stucco, sometimes in imitation of stone, and real stone has often been painted. The charm of shingle and unpainted *fer blanc* is rare, having been replaced by asphalt shingle, and extensions have been added without a thought of harmonizing with the existing house. Faded colour has sometimes given way to new paint, the blatancy of which is a shock to the mellowness of ancient walls. Some of the honest walls have actually been covered with sheets of asphalt siding, made to imitate brick or coursed stone.

This book is intended to be a record, not of the houses as they are now, but as they were in their most attractive state. In my drawings, some trees have been removed to show the buildings more clearly, and some trees and bushes have been added – where possibly they once grew – all in the interests of doing justice to the houses.

I feel, finally, that a word should also be said about the *inhabitants* of the houses. It is said that true architecture reflects the character of its designers. These houses have a simple greatness. Their simple mass, their sensible roofs, their orderly pattern of windows, are all straightforward and bold. They reflect the directness and boldness of the inhabitants – men and women who came to the wilderness of New France with the zeal of the pioneer, the faith of their fathers, and the strength born of self-confidence. Even when forsaken by the government of their homeland, they fought on against Indians, Englishmen, and the elements, the worst of which was winter – incomparably more severe than any they had ever experienced in France.

It is unthinkable that such architecture should be allowed to perish through neglect. It is the only truly Canadian architecture we have in this great country.

The Houses

This is probably the oldest house in Canada. It was started in 1637, but in June 1657 it was destroyed by fire. As the stone walls were still standing, and in good repair, the reconstruction was started immediately. The front, which faces the St Lawrence River, is of stone, and is symmetrical about a centre doorway, which is emphasized with a classical cornice and pilasters. The gable wall and chimneys are also of stone, covered with clapboard. The chimney of the one-storey addition has been carried up beside the main chimney, encased in clapboard together. Those who admire the character of stonework are opposed to covering it with wood, but the early settlers had no cement. Their mortar was only sand and lime, which is neither strong nor weatherproof. Rain would seep into the mortar, which would freeze and break – hence the boarding, to keep out the rain. In 1924 the Dobell family, owners of this house, gave it to the Province.

This house was built between 1673 and 1708 and was first known as Berthier manor, being owned by Captain Isaac Berthier (1638-1708) of the Régiment de l'Allier, a farmer of some substance and esteem. The building is entirely sheathed with vertical boarding on the lower storey. The roof and gables are covered with wooden shingles and most of the window-panes are early, small ones. The view shown is of the rear, but the entrance front is equally picturesque.

Built by Jean Mourier between 1678 and 1680, this house has the pavilion type of roof brought over from France. The verandah was probably added in the nineteenth century, but it seems to enhance the charm of this attractive building. The superimposed dormers at the end of the roof are small and unusual, but the simple finials at the ends of the roof-ridge are traditional to this type of dwelling.

Eight generations of the Villeneuve family lived on this property before 1927; the first arrived in 1684. This house has the earliest type of roof, the pavilion, which originally was built with small eaves. The eaves on front and back have probably been extended, and the verandah on the front was added about 1900. The number of dormers on the rear has been changed from two to three, their roofs have been changed from hipped to gabled, and the window-panes from small to large.

This drawing shows the house as it was originally built, in 1688 or thereabouts. Later additions included a verandah and new dormers. Trees, which cover Westmount, have been kept well back from the house in this view: early settlers usually cleared the land near the house of trees, for they 'attracted' lightning and could hide Indians. When this building was purchased by the Canadian Heritage of Quebec in 1960, it was badly in need of repairs – four of the six knee-braces of the three cross-trusses had been removed by various generations of the Hurtubise family, who still owned it. In building it, the chimneys were set to one side of the main ridge to lessen the probability of setting fire to the longitudinal truss that spans from gable to gable. There are three loop-holes on the south side of the basement, in case of Indian attack, and a two-foot-thick wall down the centre. The only access to the north half of the basement, where the women and children would take refuge, was through a seven-inch-thick trapdoor in the kitchen floor.

This is probably the most rewarding of all the historic buildings that are open to the public in the Montreal area. The property of the Sisters of the Congregation de Nôtre Dame for over three hundred years, it was restored as a Centennial project in 1967, and has been furnished with genuine antiques under the guidance of Jean Palardy. It is situated near the Marguerite Bourgeoys Park, just east of the north end of the Champlain Bridge, downstream from the Lachine rapids.

The original wooden farmhouse which stood on the site, bought from François Le Ber in 1668, was burned. The central block of the existing building, once two-thirds of its present length, was built in 1698, and the two end-blocks supposedly in 1726 and 1728, after the danger of Indian attack was almost over. The main block contains probably the most impressive piece of timber roof construction in the Montreal area. It was built two storeys high to the eaves, because it stood about two miles outside the walled town and was therefore especially vulnerable to attack by Indians – whose favourite method of destroying buildings was to set light to the eaves with torches. In the sketch, the main door has been moved back to its original position, in the centre of the façade. The bell-turret, once on the centre of the original 1698 building, has not been so moved. It was in this house that the *filles du Roi* were received by Marguerite Bourgeoys and housed until they were married to the settlers.

The drawing is of the rear of the house and shows how satisfying an unsymmetrical design can be – if the building fits into the hillside and the dormers and chimneys are symmetrical. The house was built before 1700; the site was granted to Michel Lecourt before 1655. The house owes much of its firm character to the high roof.

This house was probably built about 1700 and occupied by British troops in 1759. The design shows how haphazard the openings in the lower storey can be, if the dormers above are equally spaced and delicate in detail. Most of the old farm-houses of the Island have centre chimneys of stone. The builder of this one refrained from adding two false chimneys at the ends of the roof, as many local farmers were wont to do.

This large and dignified dwelling was built in 1718, according to the inscription which was once over the door. It was destroyed by fire in 1926, a few months after it was measured, photographed, and recorded by the architectural students of McGill University. It measured 81 feet by 32 feet. The exterior wall was 12 feet high, and the ridge of the roof rose another 24 feet above that. The huge roof with its three insignificant dormers had immense dignity. The loss to architecture in the Province was immense.

This house, north of the old Montreal-Quebec road, is unusual in having two rows of dormers, and three stone chimneys. It suggests how aesthetically unnecessary it is to have an equal number of windows on each side of the front door, if the dormers are set symmetrically in the roof. The strong line of the deep eaves makes it unnecessary to have centre-lines carry up from one storey to another.

This house owes much of its serenity to the length of its roof, which covers not only the living quarters but the vehicle shed as well. The symmetrical placing of small dormers in this all-embracing roof mass allows a considerable variety of openings in the ground storey without loss of dignity to the whole. The ox-cart is shown as a record of the old days – 1921 – in which the author made the original sketch, but oxen may still be seen on the Island today.

This little house has as charming lines as can be found in the Province of Quebec, and shows the earliest form of roof – a single slope without dormers, valleys, or bell-cast eaves. Unlike other gabled houses, this one has finials at the end of the roof-ridge. These are usually found in pavilion roofs only. The massive chimney and the fenestration of the gable-end are particularly appealing.

This building – in the opinion of the author – is possibly the most charming erected during the French régime in Canada. It was built in 1717 as a residence for the priests of the adjoining church. The east block was added to and the west block built in 1725, when it became a fort. About forty per cent of the original wall of the fort is still standing. Like all old buildings in this country, it has suffered a number of alterations, but in 1972 a certain amount of interior restoration was carried out, and the main hall was immensely improved thereby. One's first impression is of an architect-designed manor brought over from northern France. Its builders had in mind the Indians who were converted to Christianity, and it now fittingly belongs to the Department of Indian and Northern Affairs. This view is from the south. The St Lawrence Seaway forms the northern boundary of the property.

This house, easily the largest on the Island, was built by Jean Mauvide, probably about 1734. It still bears the scars of cannon balls from Admiral Saunders' British fleet, when the Island was attacked by Wolfe's forces in 1759. The drawing shows the house as it probably appeared when it was being restored by Judge Pouliot in 1928. The walls are of stone, covered with stucco, and the surrounds of the windows are of cut-stone. The round finials at the ends of the roof-ridge are more sophisticated in design than the tapered 'stakes' of the cottages. The entrance door-frames are reserved Classic, as is the moulded cornice under the eaves. The curved braces in the pediments of the dormers are reminiscent of the 'half-timber work' of Normandy.

Sagging eaves and bowed ridge attest to the age of this house, built about 1747, and extended by twenty feet in 1792. The lower windows are shown with the usual twenty-four panes of the French régime. The dormers have twenty panes instead of the usual sixteen. The walls are covered with vertical boarding. The ground floor is only just above ground level on this side. Note that the dormer roofs are hipped instead of being gabled, as they usually were. The roof, which is pavilion in style, probably had simple finials at the end of the ridge, as was the custom.

This house could not be recognized from the drawing, so much has been changed. The large end-chimneys have been removed, and a large dormer and a columned verandah have been added to the façade, the wall of which has been covered with stucco lined in imitation of cut-stone joints. The once-unbroken surface of the steep roof and the parapet-gables must have had great dignity. The house predates the English occupation.

This house was built about 1750 and partly destroyed by the war of 1759. It is a double house, symmetrical on the south front except for one dormer. This, the rear façade, is symmetrical also, except for the most easterly window, and gains additional dignity from its location at the top of a slight rise. The stone walls have been covered with stucco on front and rear, with clapboard on the gables.

This is a double house, built of wood, and has the early pavilion type of roof with small eaves. Window-sash have been changed from twenty-four panes per opening to six panes – a common practice. The massive stone chimneys lend a sense of hospitality to the long, dignified structure. The stone-fronted root-house extends above the grade, an unusual construction – they more often were completely buried.

This, one of the outbuildings belonging to the house of the Hon. Pierre Boucher, built in 1760, has several unusual features. It has the only *oeil-de-boeuf* (round window), the only dormers with shutters, and the only ground-floor door in the gable-end, shown in this book. It also has an unusual, but pleasing, mass. Note the five small circular plates by which the stone walls are anchored to the interior tie-rods. There was once a large platform at the gable-end. The original sketch was made in 1928.

This house was built in three stages by Jean Joseph Trestler. He was of German descent, but the building is in the French-Canadian tradition. The central section is dated 1798, the west wing 1805, and the east wing 1806. Certain alterations were made–tastefully but not always traditionally–by Gustave Rainville, who recently owned the house for some years. Its total exterior dimensions are 139 by 40 feet. It has numerous dormers and large chimneys. Trestler apparently traded in furs with the Indians who came down the Ottawa River past his house on their way to Montreal, for the house contains a stone-vaulted storeroom, at ground level, 36 feet long by 24 feet wide, with numerous iron hooks in the vault for hanging furs. The original iron shutters, of a type once common to the shops and houses of Montreal, are still in evidence. Many of the windows still contain the original glass, in small panes, and many fireplaces their original cut-stone lintels, stone hearths, and tapered flues. The view shown here is of the east end, from the north side.

The drawing is of the back of the house which, unlike the front, shows no attempt at symmetry. The balance is most intriguing, and the effect is charming – reminiscent of rural England rather than French Canada. This house was built about 1800, but follows the earliest type, that of the pavilion roof. Recent changes to the front have not improved its character.

This stone house, according to Vézina family legends, served as Wolfe's headquarters in 1759. It is unusual in having only one end-chimney. Most houses in the vicinity have two, and others have one genuine stone and two false ones, in wood, at the tops of the gables. Several houses have small, square windows in the dairies, as is shown here. The house was lengthened about seventy-five years ago.

Architecturally this house is a milestone. The earliest type of roof style had been pavilion, that is hipped, with ends of a much steeper slope than the front and back. Gradually the slope became still steeper, until in this house and a few others it became almost vertical – in fact, a gable. These shingled neo-gables have dormers that have so slight a projection from the roof surface that they are hardly more than drawn on. The fanciful, fretted pediments over the windows are unusual, and were probably added when the small window-panes – usually six in the height of the sash – were changed to three.

This is an early house with a pavilion roof, complete with simple finials, *fer blanc* roof covering, and – a very unusual feature in so small a house – two rows of dormers. The horizontal panes and flat roofs of the upper dormers suggest that they were later additions, as in fact were all dormers in the earliest houses – for the attic would normally be unoccupied until an expanding family necessitated more bedrooms, and therefore windows. *Fer blanc* was a slightly tinned metal sheet, laid with sloping butt-lines to assist drainage, said to have been made from the flattened linings of tea-cases or bully-beef tins. Slight rusting on the shiny surface made it look like gold. Most of these roofs have now been painted.

This is a small house, but the builder took immense care to make it beautiful. Most gabled houses with pitched roofs have straight rafters, sometimes with curved pieces added at the bottom to give a bell-cast four or five feet long, but the curve of this roof extends almost from top to bottom – a tiresome job of cutting. Like many houses on the Island, this one has two false chimneys at the ends of the roof. Only the centre chimney is of stone. The dormers have hipped roofs, in the early manner, and the top row of shingles under the dormer-eaves are triangular, a method of decoration common in the older houses.

This house is very symmetrical and very dignified. The proportions of doors and windows to roof and wall surfaces, the massive double chimneys, delicate dormers and large, bell-cast eaves make it an architect's delight. Clarence Gagnon, RCA, an outstanding authority on French-Canadian buildings and customs, has agreed that this is the finest house of its kind. A handsome stand of maples in front of this house – omitted in my sketch – makes it difficult to see the actual building except in winter. The seignorial mill, on the river close by, has long been a ruin.

This building, shorn of all its window-sash and doors, has been included to show the 'immaculate charm' of which even a ruin is capable – if once it was designed with an eye to satisfying proportions. The length compared to the breadth, the voids to the solids, the roof-surface to the wall-surface, all are eloquent expressions of strength and serenity, simplicity and honesty.

This is one of the long houses which included a vehicle shed under the main roof. Here the shed door is surrounded by four small, square windows, forming a playful pattern. Again the dormers are equally spaced in the long roof, giving an orderliness to the design. The end-chimneys are false – merely status symbols. The small window-panes, six high in the lower storey and five high in the upper, are of original glass, not clear enough for a good view, but with the slightly curved surface caused by the mould into which the glass was blown.

This long, dignified house was built by the Paré family, several generations of which occupied it. The projection of the roof at the gable ends is unusually large, possibly designed to cast the same deep shadow as is cast by the eaves, which is so much admired by artists. The end chimneys are false – constructed in imitation of those on Quebec City houses – but here they seem appropriate. The widely spaced windows and the rather rich classic doorway, set in the spacious white wall, are reminiscent of more tropical climes, but large windows are a mistake in the Canadian climate. They are too cold in winter and too hot in summer.

This huge house was built by the uncle of Sir George-Étienne Cartier, between 1779 and 1782. Several changes have been made since then, but it still retains most of its considerable dignity. Though far removed from the city – with its danger of fire from adjoining houses – it possesses thick, stone, gable-parapets, possibly intended to confer additional dignity to an imposing mass.

This house, birthplace of Sir George-Étienne Cartier of Confederation fame, was destroyed by fire in 1906. It was capable of housing more than one family, and its verandah, continuous along the whole front, made for sociability. The second-storey door in the end-wall is a little puzzling. Perhaps a small gallery, for use by an invalid confined to the bedroom-storey, was intended but never built. The two gable-chimneys, separate here, are usually joined into one large mass of stone, as in the Joseph Cartier house in the same village. This huge house was built about 1780.

Several houses near the Montreal-Sorel road are blessed with these wide chimneys, which have an hospitable as well as a monumental character. This is probably the most easily recognized feature of the old Quebec houses. The flues are tapered from wide at the bottom to small at the top, unlike ours today, which are of the same cross-section all the way up. Note how the façade is made to appear symmetrical by the orderly placing of dormers and verandah roof-posts. The front door is not really in the middle. Note also the second-storey door in the gable. Whether it was intended to open into a small gallery, or whether it was directly below a crane-beam used for loading grain into the top storey, can only be guessed today. In several old farmhouses, grain was stored in the attic before the space was converted into bedrooms for a growing family. Wags call such an aperture a 'mother-in-law door,' for obvious and facetious reasons.

This house is an example of the 'Ottawa valley' type, which has a hipped roof of equal slope on all sides, and a verandah on three or more sides. This type is found in many locations far from the Ottawa Valley – even as far south as St Louis, Missouri. Dormers are seldom found in these homes because of cramped headroom in the attic. Verandahs were seldom added to houses before 1800.

This edifice was built in 1810 by Paul Urgèle Valois, a descendant of Jean-Baptiste de Valois, who founded the nearby village of Valois in 1723. It stands on the Lakeshore road – once the highway between Montreal and Toronto. The façade is of cut-stone, but the building is rubble stone elsewhere. It has two groups of two dormers instead of four, equally spaced. The half-octagonal kitchen at the east end is unusual, and charming. Nowadays the building is a yacht clubhouse, appropriately near the shore of Lake St Louis.

This sturdy, beautifully proportioned house, now covered with white clapboard and with roof and dormers covered with metal, is said to have been built *pièce sur pièce* – that is of squared logs, laid one on top of another, with logs dovetailed together at the corners. In the drawing, the house is shown without clapboard or metal covering. The present owners believe that the original house was built about 1800, but considering that there is a larger Pouliot house up the hill which was built in 1667 by Samuel Pouliot, and that the Pouliot family has been well established in St Laurent for over three hundred years, this house may be still older. The dimensions of wood used in the old houses are now the envy of many modern builders. The main beams in this house are thirty feet long, and the pine floor-boards of the upper storey are eighteen inches wide. The stone foundation walls are three feet thick. The covering of the exterior walls with clapboard in 1948 has made it difficult to ascertain which of the three methods of *pièce sur pièce* construction was followed. Much of the original glass – slightly curved from the bottle-mould – is still in the windows.

This wide-gabled building, which once housed both mill and living quarters, was destroyed in the early part of the century. Where there are two symmetrical chimneys in the gable-end of a French-Canadian house, they are usually joined by a flat-topped wall, even though such a resulting width might be over thirty feet, as in the Château de Ramezay. In this, a strictly utilitarian building, they remain separate.

This dignified house was built in 1818, but still has the small panes of the earlier houses. Both the front and the gable-end are symmetrical and the dormers are well-placed in the great roof. The house has parapet gables – a device originally intended to stop the spread of fire when one house adjoins another, as in the towns. When, as in this case, such parapets are found in the open country, it indicates the builder's admiration for things urban. The large, wrought-iron S's on the gable-ends are a means of tying together the stone wall and the large timber plate on which the rafters rest.

This house was built in 1821 by a parish priest, Abbé de la Blouterie. The curve of the bell-cast roof is unusually large and handsome, and all the architectural features – large chimneys, well placed dormers, satisfying fenestration, and delicate verandah trellis – make this an unusually sophisticated architectural gem.

This was not a typical French-Canadian house. Its inspiration was obtained from the formal Classicism of two Scottish architects, the brothers Adam. It was a charming little building, one storey high in cut-stone and wood, monumental in mass and delicate in detail. Unfortunately it became empty, and because the federal government thought it might then harbour escaped criminals from the nearby penitentiary, it was demolished. The loss was irreparable.

Thomas Chapais, brother of Hon. Jean Charles Chapais, one of the Fathers of Confederation, built this house about 1840. The soffit (underside) of the eaves is curved to merge with the wall in the Gaspé tradition, giving added support as well as grace to the bell-cast roof. Faultless proportioning and spacing of windows, complete symmetry of design, and original glass in the window-sash, make this house a tasteful mixture of French-Canadian and English Colonial architecture.

This house was built about 1830 and was, therefore, a return to the earliest form – a pavilion-roofed building with small eaves. This, then, is a case of eclecticism carried out with taste, and following a national tradition. The façade is completely symmetrical except for the chimney, which is not in the centre: the location of the fireplaces made such a position impossible. The orderly windows clustered round the central, pedimented doorway, leaving blank spaces on either side, make this one of the most successful house designs in the Province. The stone dairy, on the right, is charming also.

In this house, the underside of the eaves is curved by continuing the clapboard of the walls upward and outward. In conjunction with the bell-cast curve of the roof above, this produces a graceful profile to the gable-end. The amount of work involved in building a curved framework for such refinements was not shirked by the old-time farmers. They believed in beauty, even though its attainment consumed much precious time. There are a few other examples of this curved soffit to the eaves – the Manoir Chenest at Cap-Saint-Ignace, built in 1820 (see *Encyclopedie de la Maison Quebecoise*, page 308) and the Chapais house at Rivière Ouelle, 1840 (page 102).

Lack of knowledge about the history of this house – one of many once standing beside the Côte Vertu road – must be accepted as the wages of 'progress.' Its splendid massing, its monumental chimneys, and its fine, unbroken roof are architectural attributes which deserve to be remembered. This sketch was made in 1928.

This is one of the most picturesque mills in the Province, and is still operating for the use of the local farmers. As in most old-time mills, the living-quarters of the miller are in the top storey. The mill-wheel is large and efficient, for there is a considerable drop from head-race to tail-race; the back wall is consequently about four or five storeys high. This wall was badly damaged about a century ago by an earthquake, which split a number of large stones. The Canadian Heritage of Quebec, which owns the building, has had to do a considerable amount of rebuilding and strengthening to prevent complete collapse.

I remember visiting this mill with Clarence Gagnon in 1939, when it stood beside the road that was the main highway to the Laurentian mountains north of Montreal, and Gagnon pointing out the grinding machinery – all, including cog-wheels, of hardwood – which he used to watch as a boy. The rectangular building measured 32 feet by 42 feet, and the mill machinery was worked by the water power of the Rivière aux Chiens until the introduction of electricity. It was built about 1816 by the seigneur, a Mr Monk, and it was pulled down about 1946.

This house was built by Dr Basile Charlebois, a native of Vaudreuil, in approximately 1820. He had studied medicine in Montreal and Philadelphia, and practised in Vaudreuil from 1817 to 1839, when he left to live in Montreal. For some time thereafter this house was occupied by the Jesuit Fathers and later by the Soeurs du Bon Conseil. It is now the Club Nautique, on the Lake of Two Mountains. The building has a fine cut-stone façade, composed of marble, granite, sandstone, and limestone in several colours, with bevelled edges throughout. Some of the faces have deteriorated with the weather. The cut-stone, moulded corbels at the foot of the gable-parapets are finely designed. The roof has *fer-blanc* covering and extends to cover the verandah on the south side, as shown in the drawing. A one-storey stone shed at the back is an integral part of the house. The wooden kitchen on the east end was evidently added at a somewhat later date, for its roof cuts across the cut-stone trim of the upper windows of the main house. The kitchen windows, as well as the main house, have original bottle-glass panes, which suggest that they were once in the east gable of the main house. Verandahs were not usually contemporary with a parapet-gabled house, and their roofs started separately, below the main house eaves. In this case, main and verandah roofs seem to have been built together.

Built in 1845 and known as the Turcot house, this is an elegant example of the Ottawa Valley type. This style owed its development to the popularity of the verandah, which was probably introduced from the south at the end of the eighteenth century and often occurred on at least three sides of the house. The result of this innovation, from a roofing standpoint, was a large rectangle, and the only graceful solution was a hipped roof of low pitch, as in the illustration. The airy, lattice-work supports for this roof, the symmetrical placing of chimneys and windows, and the deep shadows cast by the wide verandah roofs, followed as additional benefits to the senses.

This view, from a sketch made in 1948, shows the back of the house. The still-older road probably ran past the front – the south side. The simplicity of the roofs, dating from pre-dormer times, reinforces the considerable dignity of the grouping of masses and the placing of chimneys. Ladders were frequently placed on the roof beside a chimney in the older houses as a safety measure, because a continuous fire in the fireplace or stove below was capable of igniting the wooden roof. This ladder, reaching from ground to ridge in one flight, is unusual.

This house was not built by Simon Fraser but was bought by him when his own house, on the Lake of Two Mountains near by, burnt down in about 1812. He, being an important man in the fur trade, wished to live near the rapids at Ste Anne's, to keep an eye on the fur-laden canoes and other craft coming down the Ottawa River on their way to Montreal. (This Simon Fraser was not the one who discovered the Fraser River in B.C.). The original house was probably built about 1800, and legend has it that Thomas Moore, the Irish poet, wrote 'The Canadian boat song' while staying there. His description certainly assures us that he knew the spot well.

The drawing, made from an old photograph, shows the house as it was about one hundred years ago, while the parapet-gables, the eastern porch, and the three dormers were still in place. These dormers were removed and four Victorian ones were inserted in the spaces between. The south porch was probably added when the Gothic revival style was popular in England. In fact the plan of the house was once English, with a central stair-hall. The present stair is tucked away in the northwest corner, and may have been so placed when the house was a bank, from 1906 to 1952. The Canadian Heritage of Quebec bought and partially restored the building in 1966, when long-forgotten fireplaces, window-seats, and a recessed cupboard were exposed again. The hewn truss-work in the attic follows the French-Canadian tradition as does the *fer-blanc* roofing, which is still in place under the modern asphalt shingles. The ground floor is now a restaurant, run by the Auxiliary of the Victorian Order of Nurses, and has considerable historic atmosphere.

Index